TO Louise & Bob,
Two incredibly wonderful
People ... Thank-You f...
your Kindness and li...
You truly are one of...
greatest creations...

Love,
Your New Friends
Larry & Grateful Gail 2/201...

MW00909299

Reflections from the Heart

Reflections from the Heart

Larry Gudith

VANTAGE PRESS
New York

FIRST EDITION

Copyright © 2008 by Larry Gudith

Published by Vantage Press, Inc.
419 Park Ave. South, New York, NY 10016

Manufactured in the United States of America
ISBN: 978-0-533-15770-9

Library of Congress Catalog Card No.: 2007902274

0 9 8 7 6 5 4 3 2 1

To Gail, the love of my life,
because of you I see both sides of the sun

Contents

Reflections from the Heart

Destiny

Do I dare lift my eyes to search into
yours? . . . Are you the one who will
carry me away in the deep and roaring
riptides of your soul? . . . Just as
the sea pulls 1000 grains of sand
from the shore . . . will you pull
me to you?

I feel your arms reaching out to soothe
and reassure me, that no matter what
happens . . . whether we came together for
a season . . . a reason . . . or for a lifetime,
we will be better for it.

Falling Star

Nighttime and alone, I gazed up into the
darkness and saw a Falling Star. Perhaps
that Falling Star was a teardrop from the
Moon and together we were sharing our
loneliness.

As I watched, a tear trickled down my cheek
and I wondered if that Falling Star was one,
that at one time, you and I had wished upon.

If you're out there, Sweetheart, please catch
that Falling Star and bring it back to me,
maybe we can wish again.

100

If you live to be a hundred . . . I want to live to be a hundred minus one day . . . so I never have to live a day without you.

Last Night

Last night I took you on a picnic in the Sky
and wrapped you in a velvet blanket of Stars.
The Heavens sang your praises, while the Planets
toasted your beauty.

A Comet came along and lifted us into a Rainbow
and as we strolled hand-in-hand the Colors
saluted our love.

As we were walking I realized that there was no
Pot-of-Gold at the end . . . for my treasure was
standing next to me.

The Sand

Strolling alone on the beach, as the shore waits
to embrace the rushing surf. In the distance the
faint sound of a gull, as he searches the horizon
for his lost love.

I look down at my footprint and glance over my
shoulder remembering you rushing towards me, but
today it was not to be. Yet my heart remembers the
time we made a pair of footprints in the sand.

I truly miss you, but even the shore must let go
of the surf.

Wonder

Did you ever wonder if the Sun and Moon were competing or do you see the Sun and Moon as Lovers?

Did you ever wonder if the Stars really aren't Stars and don't sparkle or maybe the Sun and Moon with the glow of their love are merely poking holes in the sky to let the universe know of their oneness?

Did you ever wonder if the Wind is the Sun and Moon whispering their love to each other? . . . One thing I don't wonder about is the Sun and Moon's light ever fading and neither will the light in our love.

Both Sides

To love and be loved is to
feel the Sun from both sides . . .

Every Time

Every time your fingers have found mine
my heart races . . . Every time my hand
has touched your beautiful face my soul
has soared.

Every time our bodies have united I know
we're living complete oneness and total
love.

For every time we have touched is imprinted
deep within my heart and forever etched in
my soul.

Good-Bye

As the tears flowing down my cheeks kept pace
with the raindrops cascading down my window, I
realized we had shared our last memory.

Please know I will forever see your beautiful
smile in the sunlight and crave your perfect
body in the moonlight.

I know the Wind will whisper your name to me,
but I also know the time has come for you to
be free.

Keep in your heart all that we've shared, be
warm, safe, and happy for I'll always care.

Loving You

Loving you has become as natural as breathing.
I have read of love, written about love, dreamed
of it, searched for it and cried alone for it,
now in you I have found it.

When I look at you, I see all the dreams I have
ever had, each wish that I've ever wished and all
the hope for tomorrow.

Please know that as I quietly thank God each day
for my life . . . in the same whisper I thank him
for the miracle of you.

Memories

Last night, the evening shadows couldn't close
my eyes, only my teardrops could. As I lay on
my bed the long roller coaster night only carried
memories of you and I.

Flashes of your beautiful face and perfect body
only intensifies my longing to see your radiant
smile next to my pillow.

Last night, I never knew a heart could ache so
much, but then again, didn't I say that yesterday
and the day before that?

No Stranger

I'm no stranger to the rain, had my sunshine
and my pain. Down the road when I would wonder
in the distance I could hear the thunder.

I've struggled with life and even the Devil,
fact is at times I fell to his level. With all
I've done it's hard to keep believin' that in
the end I'll ever be close to even.

But through it all I still remain, cause I'm
no stranger to the rain.

My Wish

I wish you warmth and shelter from the
winter's storm and moonbeams to brighten
even your darkest nights.

I wish for you courage when the world is
afraid. I wish for your life, more of the
gold and less of the tarnish, more of the
light and less of the shadows.

I wish for you and I hope you know, that
here is a heart and home, who loves you
more than any wish could possibly give.

My Day

This morning the dawn sent in its sunlight
and could not wake me, but the thought of
you in my arms did.

This afternoon with a gentle falling rain the
breeze tried to lift my spirits, but only the
thought of your beautiful smile did.

This evening I set a table for two, but ate
alone and yet visualizing you sitting across
from me somehow made it all right.

Tonight, I closed my eyes praying for sleep,
but the night thought differently. I laid
awake dreaming of you praying that maybe
tomorrow you could make my day complete.

Never

There will never be a day when I won't smile
a quiet smile and say unspoken thanks for you.

There will never be a day when I won't celebrate
the joy of you and thank God for letting me
discover the miracle of you.

There will never be a day when I won't need our very
special sharing . . . for there will never be a day
that you will cease being my very heart and soul.

Once

Once I was truly afraid that I'd never find
someone to really care about. I guess I wanted
perfection at least for me.

I really needed a special kind of talking, an
honest way of listening, not being afraid to
laugh or cry, fun and excitement and someone
who would lift my heart with joy and let my
spirit soar.

I guess I expected a lot, but I'm a believer
and I believed that someday someone's magic
would totally transform my life.

So, in spite of all the waiting, it's been worth
it and along the way I found out dreams really
do come true . . . because what I've always wanted
isn't a dream . . . it's you.

Our Special Love

I'm reminded of it when we're not together and
you so gently drift into my thoughts making my
heart smile and my soul sing.

I realize it when were together with others, I
look at your beautiful face, listen to your sexy
voice and can hardly wait until we're alone,
because being with you is all I really need.

I'm sure of it when I hold you near me, two people,
two hearts joined as one and I feel so complete.

Our Star

I have dreamed countless dreams of you and I
together reaching for the clouds and searching
heaven for our star.

I encountered a hundred things that I wanted to
share with you today, but unfortunately you were
not here and yet it made me appreciate you and
our times together even more.

Today, I realized why we reach for our star, that
we might know how high our dreams and love can soar.

Sunrise

Sunrise was a mere frame in time before my eyes
finally saw . . . Sundown gave me solitude to
dim my senses and push life's lonely realities
away.

Like a gentle breeze kissing the falling leaves,
thoughts of you have stirred my emotions, touched
my soul, and stimulated my greatest desires.

As the early morning Sun slowly evaporates the
evening fog, you have lifted the coldness from
my heart . . . before you, sunrise was
a time I never knew.

Rocking Love

Someday when we're old and gray and
yesterday begins to remind us of
tomorrow.

As we sit in our rocking chairs and
race each other to sleep . . . let's
not forget how much we love each other.

Seasons

As softly as a Butterfly landing on a rose, you appeared to me in the spring and my spirit like the earth came alive and bloomed.

As the Spring Breeze gently kissed the summer Wind, your captivating ways consumed me like the waves rushing to embrace the shore.

As the Summer Sun slowly turned and focused its light on the brilliance of Autumn, I reflected on your beauty and radiance and a smile swept across my face, for I knew in you I was witnessing God's most beautiful creation.

In the stillness of Winter, as the earth covers itself in a blanket of white, the snowflakes gently drifted down from heaven and I realized that there weren't enough snowflakes to count all the times I thought of you.

Seasons change . . . Spring will always turn to Summer, Fall will always turn to Winter . . . and you can always turn to me, for I will not merely love you today, but Season after Season.

Sea of Memory

Two hearts pulsating as the surf rushes to
embrace the waiting shore.

Two bodies entangled in passion and desire.
The horizon flashes with lightning, not
threatening, but applauding the love it's
witnessing.

Two hearts, two bodies and one love, as the
beauty of this moment flows out with the tide
and is forever etched in the Sea of our Memory.

Reflections

Tonight in the canyon of my soul you are with
me, maybe tonight I'm just basking in the thrill
of you or reflecting on the totality of you.

Tonight like so many others, I'm reflecting on so
many days that you were the center of times I
recall with a smile and special sigh.

Tonight, like last night, I long for the totality
of your being and the joy of your spirit next to
me . . . but then again, what night won't I?

The Road

I've traveled, toured, turned a hundred times in the road, hoping to see you rushing after me, but it was not to be. I've seen you in the very depths of my soul where time has no boundaries and yet could not reach you.

Tonight, **I** see you my dream-of-dreams and oh, how badly I desire to climb behind your eyes and see me as you do. I want to ride every word that flows from your beautiful mouth, hoping to grasp your soul, your spirit, and your essence.

I long to touch and taste the hills and valleys of your perfect body and to have our bodies entangled in **love** and in passion. I long to know the oneness of us, as you lay in my arms knowing in our hearts that yesterday's journey has led us on the same path, the road to each other.

Now when I turn in the road, my head will be facing upward thanking God for the miracle of **YOU.**

Thinking

Sometimes I sit and ask myself,
"Do I love you more than myself?"
and I answer of course I do!

Because when I think of myself,
I'm thinking about me thinking
of you.

Together

To begin a new life together does not
mean we forget the lives that each of
us leaves behind.

But, rather we should remember the
differences that brought us here and
keep the memories of what You and I
are . . . in our pursuit of what we can become together.

Tall Oak or Me?

Have you ever wondered if the Tall Oak Tree was using its leaves as a blanket to protect him from hurt or pain, or if the leaves are the Tall Oak's expression of joy displaying himself for all to see?

One day a beautiful Butterfly gently landed on my shoulder and one-by-one the leaves began to fall and I realized it was okay to be me, simply me, that I didn't need the leaves to cover me at all.

Now when I see that Tall Oak Tree I know his leaves are expressing joy reaching for the sun to be all it can be. I'll always love that Butterfly for she truly set me free.

Funny, but an Oak Tree's leaves are always the last to fall.

Totality

My thoughts always drift of memories of you,
things we've shared, the way you smile and
simply the totality of you.

When we're not together my moods come more
into play and make me yearn for the joy I
feel with you and the love I find in your eyes.

When we're not together my heart and wishes
still go out to you, wishing to share in your
smile, laughter and comfort your hurts . . .
when we're not together I seem to spend my time
wishing we were.

With You

Neither by words, song or pen, can I possibly
convey the depths of my feelings for you, but
I can tell you what I feel like when I'm with
you:

It's as if I were a bird in your hands and you
released me to soar and discover heaven . . . it's
as if I were a wave on the ocean rushing to
embrace the shore . . . it's as if I were the rainbow
proudly showing my colors to the world . . . I do
know when I'm with you I own the world.

World

To the world you may be one person, but to
one person, known as me . . . you are
the world.

Waves

Your life and mine flow into each other as
a wave flows into wave . . . unless
there is joy and love for you, there can
be no real joy or love for me.

Your Name

Early this morning I wrote your name in the sand,
but the shore released it to the waves and it was
carried out to sea.

This afternoon I wrote your name in the sky, but
the Wind paused, hugged it, and sent it to heaven.

Tonight I wrote it in my heart and that's where it
will stay forever.

You

If you were a road, I would drive all
your curves . . . If you were an ocean
I would surf your waves.

If you were a star in the sky, I would
wish upon you and wish you were mine
forever.

Vision

Some people see the Sun as only a reflection on
a mountain lake . . . You and I feel the warmth.

Some people see the Stars as being frozen against
the night sky . . . You and I see their radiance.

Some people only see flowers as a source of color
. . . You and I see their uniqueness.

Some people see a gate and proceed no further . . .
You and I see what lies beyond.

Counting

Count the Stars in the desert sky, for that's how many
days I will love you . . . Count the Wildflowers on a
Summer prairie, for that's how many ways I hope to please you.

Count the snowflakes in a winter's storm, for that's how many
times I'll be there when you need me . . . Count on me and
my love forever, for that's how long I pray we'll be together.

Blessed

We are truly blessed and fortunate to be
able to share this wonderful passage through
time and space.

Never too far apart that our hearts, souls,
and bodies do not touch. For wherever life's
journey takes us we go in love.

I will always want the best for you and that
includes me . . . not because I'm perfect,
but because I'm perfectly in love with you.

Photograph

Unable to sleep as the long rollercoaster night only carries memories of you, I glance at our photograph on the nightstand and never missed you more.

As I reached for your picture a tear trickled down my cheeks as my finger traced the contours of your beautiful face.

I gently pressed my lips to yours and while wiping the tears from my eyes placed your photograph back on the nightstand. With one more look at your wonderful smile, I wondered how God could possibly have needed you more than I do.

Me

I wish I could be all that you want me
to be. I'm not perfect nor do I pretend
to be, I am what I am, isn't that truly
the key?

So I'll keep hoping until the day you see
that no man could love you more than the
one I call me.

Best Gift

The best gift you can ever give is a hug,
one size fits all and no one ever minds
if you return it.

If I Could

If I could the world would see the beauty in your eyes.
If I could all of mankind would feel the warmth of your smile.

If I could the stars would all line up and as you passed
would bow to your radiance. If I could the fireflies would
write your name against the summer night.

If I could I'd raise my arms to the sky and push the storm
elsewhere. If I could the Morning Doves would whisper my love
for you . . . If I could, you know I would.

Sigma Street

There are Golden Apples to be picked and
bridges to build and Wild Oats to sow as
our love grows.

But, later on the other side of time, the
Apples no longer taste sweet . . . bridges
fall down, meadows turn brown, as love falls
apart in a little house on Sigma Street.

About the Author

Larry Gudith was born in Michigan. While in high school he was not only an accomplished student, but a talented and gifted athlete as well, being named All-State in two sports and earning All-American status in football.

Upon graduation, Larry decided to accept an athletic scholarship to the University of Montana where he continued to achieve in the classroom as well as the playing field. He received his degree in Business Administration and was drafted by the Oakland Raiders of the National Football League.

After two years of professional football, Larry's promising career was cut short due to injury and he started a new career in the medical consulting business. Today he serves as Director of Sales and Marketing for an international manufacturer of pet products serving the grooming industry.

Larry has two beautiful daughters, Cori and Nikki. He is a Christian and proud member of Orchard Grove Community Church. His interests include church outreach programs, athletics, tennis, landscaping, travel, boating, fishing, cross-country skiing, nature and spending quality time with his beautiful fiancée, Gail, their two schnauzers (Maxx and Woofie), and their cat, CeCe.

"I truly hope I can convey the emotions we all feel and yet can't express. The warmth and joy of love shared and that which is lost," writes the Author.

This is his first published book.